This
Colder Room

By the same author

Translations
Daybreak

This
Colder Room

Bill Milner

This Colder Room
Bill Milner

Published by the Woodlands Press
Allman's Lane, Lockley Wood,
Market Drayton, TF9 2LX

ISBN 978-0-9572717-2-2

Acknowledgements:

Part of "Reading Ceramics" appeared in *HQ Poetry Magazine*.
Many of the other poems first appeared in *Keele Drafts*.

Cover Design, Page Layout and Printed by
Creative Digital Printing, Shrewsbury, Shropshire SY3 5DD
Tel: 01743 263030

Contents

Poetica

Fanfare for the Common Tongue

We sing your praises none too frequently
you wood or stone or metal of the mind;

like wooden platters once the norm
your humdrum serves our needs day-in, day-out

but on occasion you can rise, and rival
with your hammered, empty air
all types of noble artifice:

like Epstein finding in the alabaster block
athletic Adam with his head flung back
and all that is not needed cut away;

or Henry Moore, from dross and meltdown
forming a king, a queen beside him too,
sharing the spare, sufficient throne,
unmoving, hieratic and serene.

Stanza

This ancient room available for hire –
ten by fourteen – no bigger than a cell –
where many poets frequently retire
because they know that here they can write well:
there's always someone waiting at the door
to step inside, into the atmosphere
redolent of those who've gone before.

No visitor could fail to be aware
the place does not accommodate excess –
what cannot fit inside must be left out.
Guests find the constraints free them to express
their thoughts and feelings – which explains, no doubt,
why other structures are no longer there
but this still stands – and will stand – fair and square.

Dad's Army

Silk purses can be made out of sows' ears:
my whole life has been spent in doing that.
The words I command are everyday words
recruited from the useful and banal –
hardly the makers of exalted verse.
Yet, disciplined, lined up, and made to march in step
the long, the short, the tall, the heavy-footed
and those light on their feet, surprisingly
(after what seems much pointless exercise),
sent out to fight the vague and downright false,
can lift themselves to unexpected heights
before they are demobbed -- dispersed
into the undistinguished crowd
to help along once more the everyday.

Lucretius: Things Unattempted yet ...

Now I will explore regions of the Muse
not trodden yet by any venturer. I revel
in reaching virgin springs and drinking deep,
plucking new flowers and forming for myself
a chaplet remarkable for being culled
from fields whence the Pierides, before,
have never veiled another poet's brow.
Firstly because I teach exalted things,
striving to extricate the human mind
from the constrictions of religion,
writing of darkest things such limpid lines
as touch all matters with the Muses' grace.
Nor is this merely useless frippery:
as doctors giving wormwood to a child
take the cup, before they offer it, and smear
thick-flowing yellow honey round the rim
so that the child is misled by the lips
and meanwhile, quite unwittingly, drinks up
the wormwood's bitter juice and though deceived
is thereby harmlessly restored to health;
so I, because all this philosophy
to novices seems largely dour stuff,
and many people may in fact recoil,
have chosen, in addressing this to you,
to couch philosophy in dulcet verse
and touch it, as it were, in doing so,
with all the mildness of the honeyed Muse
so that my lines may hold your interest
and, while you read, bring you to understand
the constitution of the universe
and how such learning has its usefulness.

Tall Order

I have seen a giant – once.
But that was years ago – at the poetry class.
His hair was anointed – a black bed of nails;
his eyes were deep-sunken, like glimmers in caves;
his ears were barn doors without any hinges;
his teeth were eroded – like a mountain range
on a planet of bone;
his hands hung loose at the ends of his arms
like children's gloves dangling on strings;
carcases on a butcher's hook
are the nearest thing to his thwacking great thighs;
and his sabot type shoes were like dugout canoes.

His head came level with the first floor window;
we kept it open for him to take part.
He carried a paving slab under his arm
and a pencil the size of a telegraph pole.
Some of us thought him a bit of a joke
like the opera singer who had to lose weight.
Then he spoke – he read out his work,
and his resonant voice thrilled the tables and chairs,
sweeping us over emotional seas:
travellers' tales, old sorrows, old joys,
the death of his tribe, the being alone:
his heart had room for all this and more,
and when his tale set us down at the end
we sat there in silence, and he disappeared
leaving us all chastened, and convinced
that we'd been born into an age of petty verse.

Epistle

Why, you ask,
  at the beginning of each line
    the upper case?

It's a convention, I reply,
  and I'm conventional.
    But, on reflection, I realize

it can't be simply that:
  I don't join crowds, I tend to swim
    against the tide.

Perhaps it's because
  in all the magazines
    I see how much the lower case

is almost de rigueur. To be conventional
  in this respect
    is therefore to rebel.

But then again, this letter proves
  (you must agree)
    that too will not suffice.

Only from 1974
  did R.S. Thomas
    abjure the upper case;

Sebastian Arrurruz
  turned his small jewels
    on capital letters

but Geoffrey Hill,
    from that time on,
        has avoided their use;

and though Carlos Williams seemed to regard
    the initial capital
        as un-American

the Vice-President of the insurance company
    even in Opus Posthumous
        preferred its lightly starched formality.

The question, Tom,
    seems to draw lines
        across careers, between great modernists.

The precedents point
    clearly
        in both directions.

Do I need
    a divided self
        to follow them both?

Why, when what I write
    in some small way
        follows in the footsteps of (and here

you can insert yourself
    all the great users of the upper case)
        should I not humbly raise the capitals

and when I sometimes want to say, with others,
  this is poetry
    as we have reinvented it

should I not then refrain?
  Each letter privileged to open a new line
    signals alignment:

the poem itself pulls away from
  or towards
    the upper case –

its kinship is proclaimed
  by its first line.
    I just do what I'm told.

Dear Bert

Four years now since your funeral
(which went according to your careful plan)
so that, this Easter Morning,
I won't disturb your busyness in church
by telling you how glad I am
that I have found another use
for your long, thin-legged, unfolding
wallpaper-pasting table.

It lay unused and dusty, folded
like an artist's plywood portfolio
until, today, I measured it
and found that I could place it in my porch,
the ideal stand for all my bedding plants –
the whole top covered with their little cells,
with all of them now gathering their strength
and growing visibly from day to day.

In just a month or two
were you to drive down as you used to do
some would be in bud, some in flower,
and there would be enough spare plants
to brighten your back yard,
and that would please me,
knowing your disease
had robbed you of your old dexterity.

But you will not come now,
nor will the phone ring with your weekend call
so I must write this down,
revise it carefully,
and read it, so to speak, into your ear,
sure that your faith in the last day
does not, in the long interim,
preclude an interest in growing things.

An Epistle

I've set myself the task
of writing an epistle – but to whom?
Letters aren't the same as other poems:
one doesn't send a letter with mere hope
that someone will be there to pick it up.
The greeting at the start spells out a name;
the farewell means the name is understood.
So I was glad this morning, when your letter came.
It gave me an occasion, an addressee
and an address complete with postal code.
Now, like a pigeon knowing its way home,
my letter will arrive on the right mat.

So far, so good: "Dear Sheila" makes a start.
The question now is what to write about.
I could of course express astonishment
that your new garden is so well designed
and fills with form and colour what was bare.
I could reflect on all the differences
between a pattern formed in bedding plants
which by November will be dull and dead
and ones in words – your own for example –
which have a longer life – and how that longer life
may trick us into thinking words endure
when every day some aged speaker dies
and takes another language to the grave.

We've quickly moved there from the shallows
to deeper water. I'll leave that theme –
except that with it we can start to see
the nature of the epistle form itself:
it is capacious, and does not prescribe --
tragedy, or comedy, or both
are quite acceptable, as are such lines

as those above – low-level, random thoughts:
"All human life," as someone says elsewhere.
I also think that, like a telephone,
a letter should transmit the writer's voice –
the intonations rising from the page
clearly, as if the sender spoke the lines.

There's more to say – and an anthology
of verse epistles down from Roman times
through every age up to the present day
would eloquently say those other things
if only some bright publisher would take
the opportunity.
                      One point the book would make
is that a letter should not be too long.
(No one likes to see their reader nod
and hear the paper slipping to the floor.)
"Best wishes" should conclude it in good time.

Some Long Lines on Long Lines

Long lines, you say . . . long lines. Would that be Walt Whitman
  or Blake?
Or Christopher Smart or that Yank whose name I forget –
  published by Bloodaxe of course . . .
or is it Carcanet? You know who I mean – the page is not wide
  enough for him:
his serpentine lines turn back on themselves and very near eat
  their own tails.
There's Eliot too in "The Rock" :
"Where is the wisdom we have lost in knowledge?
Where is the knowledge we have lost in information?" . . . but I
  see what is happening here – Something is trying to stave off
  our start.
Is the line going to lay down a subject
  or the topic determine the line?
Let's start with a subject and see where that takes us to.
Subject. Now then. What have we got in the log-pile?
Though if these lines are not already too long to retract
I'll go for a different image: my head is a fizzing beehive, a swarm of
  potential poems. I must be ruthless and get out the puffer of
  smoke
and deploy it until I have left the narrowest possible choice.
Here we are – the first two: "The Bishop";

"The Washing Machine": two epic subjects worthy of
    Homer or Shakespeare. (Think only
of Mrs. Goedheart and her mighty mangle-topped concrete-
    mixer pulled out every week in her
    glass-place in – here's the rub – '39.
There was Lancashire leading the world.)
    Hexameters ready yourselves!
As for me – it's too late – should have started decades ago,
but here comes another bee from my bonnet, long lines and
    topic together,
gift-wrapped for a topic-strapped bard: Hopkins, Manley,
    Gerard
his late, long-lined sonnets, and his Dark Night of the Soul.
That's my subject.
I'm feeling depressed already.
These long lines are going to drag.

Henry Howard, Earl of Surrey, poised to translate Virgil's 'Aeneid'

How can I do justice to this book?
We have no noble, sober forms
to take high Virgil's long lines in
when they step off translation's shaky bridge.
What Chaucer called the rim-ram-ruff of Gawain's verse
and brother Langland's sprawling work –
the tolling bells of Chaucer's constant rhyme:
neither will do.
The one has lines approximating Virgil's length
but is too rustic for his polished style;
the other jingle-jangle is quite alien
to Virgil's seamless, unrhymed paragraphs.
Yet, I think that if I discard rhyme
I still ought to retain our five-stress line.
'Our' I say because it seems to underlie
the greatest things my forebears have achieved.
Let's see. *Conticuere omnes* – **They whisted all**
Intentique ora tenebant – **with fixed face attent**
Inde toro pater Aeneas sic orsus ab alto –
when Prince Aeneas from the royal seat
thus gan to speak: "O queen, it is thy will
I should renew a woe cannot be told."

…………...

I find this line congenial: it can convey
something of the Latin's dignity.
Now that's decided I can make a start.
Let's hope I have some rest from soldiering.

Window Cleaner

The ease with which my wiper on a stick
seems to sweep whole plate glass windows clean
had to be learned. For a long time
what I thought clear from inside looking out
was far from clear to someone looking in.
Only the daily grind taught me the skill:
with quiet pride in sheer transparency
to work until the final blemish fades.

Lebenslauf

A Cautious Welcome

Little one, leaving the warmth of the womb
for this much larger, colder room –
with one breathtaking, reckless dive
now independently alive –
though Dad can dandle you all day
this pleasant task just doesn't pay.
He's young and strong and wouldn't shirk
to undertake the hardest work.

But there are no jobs to be had.
You've just arrived when times are bad
but you sleep on, my little man –
I swear we'll do the best we can
to see you well-clothed and well-fed
and keep a roof over your head.
Watching the news we're glad at least
you're here, not in the Middle East.

Seeing how children there have died
we think perhaps luck's on your side
so welcome to our mortgaged home.
It may not be a pleasure dome
but sight and sound and earth and air
are here as much as anywhere.
The world lies all before you boy,
so stretch your legs – imbibe – enjoy.

At a Christening

I wonder how the heroes got their names:
Were Hector and Achilles named like this,
Infants surrounded by their families,
Joined with a word one day for days to come?
Or were they named to please a blind man's ear
And ease the flow of his prolific verse?

This day is special, and I dare to think
That Homer too attended naming days
And, as he listened, formed a clear resolve
Never to break this lovely, fragile bond
But call his heroes by their given names
No matter how prosaic they might seem.

Night-words

The world was voluble from early days:
the intonations of his mother's voice;
the tightening of the blankets in the cot,
her final act each night before she went,
leaving, like Three Blind Mice or Jack and Jill,
Hail Marys going over in his mind;
the frequent head-lights' threatening lassos
circling his bed before he fell asleep
or didn't until after closing time
and all the men's loud voices died away;
and once, the darkest of night syllables,
the eerie crying of the neighbour's cat
injured by a vehicle's glancing blow;
and when the crying stopped, a great relief.

Catullus: Lugete ...

Mourn, Venus and all you cupids
and anyone who has a heart,
for my darling's little sparrow
has dropped down dead.
He was her pet. She loved him
and held him more precious than sight itself.
He was sweet as honey, and knew the girl
just as well as she knew her own mother.
He never moved far from out of her lap
but hopping around her he chirruped and chirped
for her sake alone: she was his mistress.

And now he has travelled that shadowy road
which none, they say, can ever retrace.
Curse your evil darkness, Death.
You bolt down everything that's beautiful.
What a crime. Poor bird.
What a beauty was lost when you took it away.
And now look what your handiwork has done.
See – how my girlfriend's eyes
are reddened and swollen with weeping.

First Loss

The common elements combine
and hold their own against decay
whether they tough it out for years
or lose the battle in a day

like this child's monster bubble
floating down the forest ride
wearing, briefly, its surroundings
on its iridescent side.

Flexing, it commands our gaze
the more because we hold our breath
knowing what is imminent:
disintegration – instant death.

But this one is too young to know;
she finds the death too much to bear,
filling with her sudden keening
all the forest's vacant air.

For Children
of any age

The Old Farmhouse

The houses on our road are nearly all the same
but while most of them have numbers there is one that has a name.
The rest are brick like ours, a sort of rusty red
but this one house is built of sandstone blocks instead.
It's called "The Farmhouse" and it must be very old.
It reminds us that we're living on the fields the farmer sold.
Where my father mows the lawn and the roses grow today
was perhaps a flower-meadow where the workers cut the hay,
and it's strange to think the place where we sit and have our meals
could have been a gateway squashed and squelched by tractor wheels
and where mother's bending down to fill the washer now
may be where the milkmaid put her stool to milk the cow.
I can see a crowd of piglets, full of mischief, who've been stealing
windfalls from the orchard, come scampering and squealing
across our posh new carpet and through the kitchen door
past the red hen scratching at the shiny parquet floor,
and I'm sure that when I'm standing on the topmost of the stairs
I'm exactly where the ladder poked through apples or through pears,

and our little square front garden with its castellated wall
was where, in bygone winters, the carthorse had his stall.
And sometimes when I lie awake, thinking in the dark,
I feel as if our houses have destroyed a Noah's Ark –
but then again, I know we can't keep everything that's old
and we might not have a home if the farm had not been sold.

Our Avenue

In winter our avenue
With trees on either side
Seems to form a guard of honour
For some bridegroom and his bride

And on my birthday every spring
It greets me with the sight
Of its chestnut trees and cherry trees
All festooned with white.

In summer its green canopy
Protecting us from heat
Scatters golden sovereigns
Enriching the whole street.

Then, gradually, the leaves turn brown
Then yellow, then they fall,
And when I'm walking through them
I think autumn's best of all.

But then comes winter once again;
I can't make up my mind.
I know that all year round I'm glad
Our avenue is lined

With these ever-changing trees.
May they never be cut down:
It's their little bit of countryside
That makes me love the town.

Our Visitor

A pheasant came into our garden today.
I think it must simply have lost its way.
We tried not to startle our beautiful guest
with his bright red cheeks and his golden breast.

As he looked around with his glass-button eyes
he seemed to be staring in some surprise
at the fences, washing lines and sheds
and our rather bedraggled flowerbeds

because he's really a country bird.
Perhaps he ran into town when he heard
his brothers and sisters being shot dead.
I hope he's not killed by a car instead.

He hasn't got very much sense, you see:
he was born a prisoner, then set free
and he's never learned like wild jays and crows
that he has to be careful wherever he goes.

He fluttered over our garden wall
and later – just once – we heard him call.
From how far away we couldn't tell.
But wherever he is we wish him well.

The Image of Man

The cheerful snowman outside on the drive –
what would he have thought if he'd come alive?
His carrot nose might have sniffed the air
and his coal–black eyes have begun to stare
first at the sky, then at the ground,
and I'm wondering whether he would have frowned
to see how the morning's smooth white sheet
untouched by wheels, untrampled by feet,
was slowly spoiled by the mess we made
as we churned up the gravel with the spade.
The more we shovelled, the more he grew,
the more the stones and the dirt showed through.

Or would he have thought, "I'd never have been
if they hadn't disturbed that original scene.
No matter how heavy the overnight fall
its blankness carried no message at all.
But I'm made in the image of man you know,
and that puts a smile on the face of the snow."

Grandpa is Old

When he grew up there were no motor cars
and the gas lamps were too weak to hide the stars.
They bought milk and eggs from the nearby farm
and he's sure it never did anyone harm;
"Just over the road," he says, and smiles
asking, "Why should milk travel so many miles?"
If he sees me going to school he jokes
and asks how it is that today's young folks
have to jump on a bus every morning and ride
what in his day he says would be called a cock-stride.
And then he stops smiling and asks did I know
that hundreds of generations ago
human beings were giants who ran with the deer
and wrestled with bears without any fear
but since then, as generations have passed,
they've got weaker and weaker until at last
from ancestors tall and sturdy as trees
we've come down to what he calls "Weak at the knees."
He gets these funny ideas in his head –
I think it's probably something he's read.
I don't argue, but I think we've made lots of gains;
we're smaller perhaps – but we've got bigger brains.
But Grandpa is Grandpa – he'll never be told.
It's always the same when people get old.

Scarecrow

I'm a cross made of sticks cut down from the wood.
I'd wipe this smile off my face if I could –
I've had it ever since I was born
when I thought I was going to protect the corn
but blow me that's not what I'm doing at all.
I'm stuck here outside the village hall
dressed up in a bowler, a suit and a tie
surrounded by houses that multiply
out of which every day the whole village pours
with a revving of engines, a slamming of doors.

Rumour has it that soon the day will arrive
when this dormer village will come half alive
all because, as if dragons' teeth had been sown,
elsewhere in the village more scarecrows have grown
part of a Grand Fun Day I hear
when some celebrity's going to appear
to declare who wins a prize for his maker.

I think it's all daft. I long for an acre
of good clammy soil – the croak of the crows –
a scruffy old coat – a stick for a nose –
just to be shut of this fiddle-de-dee
and recover my age-old "raison to be".

The Fight

There's a strange cat in our garden;
It often comes at night.
Our Mog doesn't like it –
There's going to be a fight.

They circle round each other
Like wrestlers in a ring;
Their fur stands up like bristles
And then – they start to sing.

It's not a love song either;
It's more a quiet howl
As they jockey for position
In their weird slow-motion prowl.

They arch their backs, their legs go stiff,
Their tails stand up like snakes;
Their howling rises to a wail –
And Tim, my brother, wakes

Just in time to watch with me
Their furious, momentary fight.
Fur flies – they roll and tumble –
Then the stranger is in flight.

He disappears through the hedge,
Leaving our victorious Mog
Looking pleased he's proved the stranger
Is the feline underdog.

Those Were the Days (or were they?)

I'm now very old, and when I was a child
there was never a winter that we could call mild.
At the end of November snow started to fall
and the earth seemed to turn into one big snowball.
The farmer rescuing sheep didn't know
which white was wool and which white was snow.
His dog couldn't help to bring the flock in
for the hampering snow nearly up to his chin
and the river that ran past the edge of his field
slowed down to a trickle before it congealed
and the fish felt the frost encroach like a vice
suspending their lives in a prison of ice.

There was no central heating of course in those days
but the big open fire was always ablaze.
Outside, I thought myself venturesome, bold,
a journeying knight in the Kingdom of Cold –
I think it must have been something I'd read
had worked this magic inside my head;
Gawain I guess – he had to go
through mist, and ice, and snittering snow
and through drifts, like our postman, up to his knees.
One year in fact he tried to use skis:
he'd no red van – as I ought to have said –
he had to ride Shanks's Pony instead.

As for us, summer bikes put away,
we got out the sledge (which Mum called a sleigh)
and taking turns to sit on the top
we used it to bring supplies from the shop.
Some days we'd clear a deep drift from the door
and come back to find it worse than before.
There were hardships, yes, but we didn't mind;
they were nothing compared to the horrible grind
of life in the town. The winter there
was a miserable, dirty, slushy affair.
I hated the place, and felt ready to choke
whenever I breathed in its fog, soot and smoke.

But see now, I feel myself slowing down.
When I read what I've written I can't help but frown.
Is it really all as true as it seems
or just a deceptive procession of dreams?
How is it these scenes fill my mind like a flood
when I know my memory's not very good?
I wonder, dear reader, what kind of surprise
it would be if this poem's a bundle of lies.
While you think about that, I'm calling a halt.
I suggest you stock up with a big load of salt
and spread it like doubt on the tale that I've told
because I did warn you: I am very old.

Lebenslauf 2

Tom

The whole village lined the street
   Though rain clouds filled the sky.
Even the shift worker got out of bed
   To watch the hearse go by.

It passed the terraced house which heard
   His first, lusty, welcome cry
Where, later, Mother sang to him
   And Dad read "Peacock Pie".

It passed the two-roomed sandstone school
   Where staff said he was bright
And needed little help from them
   To learn to read and write.

It passed the village playing field
   Where, winters, he kept goal
And, summers, an all-rounder,
   He could bat, and field and bowl.

It passed the well-kept village hall
   Where he had learned to dance
And when he was fifteen had felt
   The onset of romance.

And finally it passed the yard
   Of Simon Yates's farm
Where Tom the village favourite
   suffered grievous harm.

He'd crawled beneath a heavy trailer
　　To do some small repair
But he – or someone else – had taken
　　Insufficient care.

Poor lad. The prop gave way.
　　He knew that he would die
And so did all the village
　　From his scarcely human cry.

Years have passed, but old folk say
　　Mention Tom and they can hear
As chilling as the day he died
　　That cry of shock and pain and fear.

He was an only child; his mother,
　　A widow on her own,
Had only a small pension;
　　She couldn't buy a stone.

But if you go to see the grave
　　As I did in the spring
You'll find it full of primroses
　　Their buds just opening

As if to say remember Tom –
　　What died when he was killed –
Like flowers blighted by a frost
　　Such promise unfulfilled.

A Tragic Tale

(A conversation between Father and Daughter, with a
fraught interjection by Mama)

Good heavens, my dear child, what have you been doing?
I see by your pallor some trouble is brewing,
and who is that youth you have brought on your arm
who looks too anaemic to do any harm?

O Father, I swear that we said we'd agree
to call it a day when he got to my knee,
but he broke the agreement, his hand kept on rising
and rising – I found it quite hypnotizing.

My daughter, my daughter, surely you know
you can stop your old pony by just shouting 'whoa'
and ladies' long skirts, all your flounces and frills,
are designed to discourage such disgraceful thrills.

We must send you away for a year and a day.
(My nerves would not stand what the neighbours
    would say.)
We know an old woman in Strawberry Street
who's used to these things and is very discreet.

O Papa, that's too cruel. I know what you mean.
To murder the unborn is surely obscene,
and whether my child is a girl or a boy
I know it will bring me years of great joy.

You're impossible, girl. We've paid that fine school
thousands of pounds to turn out a fool.
You can leave home – That's final. I'm saying no more.
We're not giving houseroom to such a young whore.

Then farewell, my parents. Your views are so rotten
I wonder how I was ever begotten.
I'll keep my eyes open, as I scrimp and slave,
for your funerals – and I'll dance on your grave.

A Dream

I dreamed in my dream
That watery Wells

Had gone dry overnight.
No gutters ran

With rivulets.
A silence descended

Unknown before.
The council convened

But before the chairman
Could call them to order

Wells disappeared
Off the screen of my mind

And I saw instead
Like a whale of a mole

The truant waters
Shouldering east

Till they settled round
And a good depth below

The Ship of the Fens.
Then that wonderful work

Began to capsize
With a list to starboard.

The bishop, recalled
From a tropical beach,

Arrived back still sporting
Gaudy off-duty gear

And mounted to what
He called his bridge

And through a loud-hailer
Addressed the crowd

Saying he was no cowardly
Pleasure cruise captain.

He would stand at his post
Until the last wafer

The final bottle
Of communion wine

Had been snatched from the jaws
Of a watery grave.

He then announced
To gasps from the crowd

That he had not wasted
His time on the plane:

He'd put to good use
His ecclesiastical

Bang-up-to-date
Holy mobile

To speak to Lord Rogers
Of Lloyd's Building fame

And ask him to design
A new cathedral

Entirely of tin
And about the size

Of an average semi.
"The faithful are only

A handful these days.
Why should we build

For tourists to gawp at?
Let the Chinks with their

No doubt top of the range
Snooping cameras

Go somewhere else."
His Worship was clearly

Carried away
But correctness

Was never
A strong point of his.

I think I can already
Hear you asking

What did his boss
The Archbish have to say.

And I'm sad to report
That just as he opened

The door of his palace
And then his mouth

To speak to reporters
I was jolted awake

By my jangling alarm.

★★★★★★

Just a dream you say.

Nevertheless
Some dreams come true.

I fear for Ely
And tremble for Wells.

A Man's Life

"Bible puncher! Virgin soldier! Queer!"
"You grab 'is arms . . . God, talk about thick!"
And then the retchings after drinking beer
they forced on him because it made him sick.

After a childhood in an orphanage
where, lucky in misfortune, he was taught
the ways of kindness, frightened to engage
what seemed to him a hostile world, he sought

the shelter of another institution.
It gave him hell. He tried. A witness said
after a sordid fight in the ablution
he took karate lessons, shaved his head,

but still he died, learned though ESN
in nasty things about his fellow men.

Words for a Golden Wedding

I can say that I'm honoured to be here
Because you'll know what I mean:
It has nothing to do with wealth or fame
Or the peerage and the Queen.

It has to do with shared values:
I'm pleased to think that you know
I treasure the things that you do —
Things that words, though I love them, can't show.

You can say you love one another.
I can say I can stand on my head.
But time is the great assayer
Who asks you to prove what you've said.

He tests and interrogates,
Throws all that he's got in your way,
Invites you to break your word,
Suggests that you call it a day.

And as often as not he succeeds:
Like physiques that are sturdy and hale
The very best will in the world
Can be battered and bruised and then fail.

But you've shown him where to get off
And like makers of excellent wine
Shown – used wisely – as well as destroy
We can teach him how to refine.

The years have proved that you meant it
When you said, "to have and to hold".
You've taken the rough as well as the smooth
And polished it all into gold.

And we hope this occasion will seem
Just a sort of invisible door
Through which you will pass from your fifty years
To share, and enjoy, many more.

Chanson

We stand on the Millennium Bridge. Below
pleasure boats and barges come and go
    and underneath our feet
the river's shifting waters ebb and flow.

> *The city's clocks announce the hour.*
> *One pledge can nullify time's power.*

The old forget what young ones understand –
that simply joining faithful hand to hand
    can make us strong
as this bridge safely joining land to land.

> *The city's clocks proclaim the hour.*
> *Our pledge has nullified time's power.*

***

We're older now and see our sad mistake.
We never thought our solid earth could quake.
    It did. Love died:
even the strongest bridges sometimes break.

> *The city's clocks insist upon the hour.*
> *Can any pledges nullify time's power?*

> *Time passes . . . briefly we remain,*
> *seizing its joy, enduring its pain.*

Last Word

You say my company is your idea of Hell – Me
You call devil. Were we at war, I think you'd kill me.

Were I a tree, planted for your delight
Would you not scorn the gift, and fell me?

Were I a mist like a protective veil
Thrown round your shoulders, you would dispel me.

Were I a fountain cooling your court-yard
You would prefer the heat and quell me.

Were I an heirloom crafted in fine gold
You'd treat me as a worthless thing and sell me.

To me it's you who are fine gold – I never knew
Beauty had such power to compel me.

I do not want to leave, I cleave to you.
You stamp your foot – open the door – expel me.

So many grievances you say you have
Yet when I ask you what they are, you never tell,

And since you are ice no body-heat can melt
There's only one word left, my Rose: farewell.

Al Fine

The old composer sitting up in bed,
the man through whom a nation found itself,
pushes aside his plate, puts earphones on his head,
and takes a record from a bedside shelf.

The adagio begins: he feels again the pride
invested in the first impulsive draft,
and traces, till the final chords have died,
the discipline that impulse owes to craft.

But all his joy in making is now past:
he knows this sombre work will be his last.
A barren silence overwhelms his life.

He falls asleep, surrounded by his scores,
surrenders to self-pity, and ignores
the patient ministrations of his wife.

Bleak Domain

Sick in the bleak domain of neither-nor,
he thought how different his life had been
back in the happy days of either-or

forgetting that those stern alternatives
had never salved the wounds of memory,
replete with pristine moments of both-and.

Last Canvas

It was Arcadia of a kind:
a painting by a man resigned
to knowing that he may well die
before the paint had time to dry.
There was a country through the frame,
a glowing country with no name,
apparently without a town,
flooded with light at sun-go-down.

A big field had been closely shorn
of, perhaps, some kind of corn
but those who'd harvested the yield
had gone – had strewn across the field
old implements: scythe, sickle, rake
finer than those of modern make.
An idle cart, too, stood nearby,
shafts pointing to the cloudless sky.

There was a road. It went nowhere,
but climbed and seemed to end in air.
No footfall must have passed to raise
this highway's dust for days and days,
and by its side huge oak trees made
a wide, inviting, deep, cool shade
offering a whole herd retreat
from the fierceness of the heat.

To me it seemed there was a rare
visual silence everywhere
as if all nature held its breath
aware of his impending death,
while – by the last brush-strokes he made –
a hill-top, sandstone church conveyed
an unheard benediction, tolled
over an evening bathed in gold.

Mourir

My wife will visit me again tonight
to feed me soft emulsion of egg-yolk,
and once again my taste-buds will evoke
sad memories of sensual delight

as if they were no part of the me that knows.
My watch-strap rattles loosely round my wrist,
a bracelet of bright metal, and my toes
have gone already. I must try to insist

Maintenant que je ne suis qu'un squelette
(Ah, my French! What things come to our aid!)
our grandchild stay away now – I'm no sight
for happy little children, I'm afraid.

But then the new nurse makes me catch my breath –
my daughter's age . . . Will I be her first death?

The Wharf

It looks man-made: a cutting through the fields,
a landing-stage worn hollow over time,
a fetid breeze making the little boat

perform its tethered arc.
There is no ferryman about;
he may be resting in his cabin there

slurping at his billy-can of tea.
One day I'll come to find him stepping in,
opening his greasy leather purse

and smiling, pleased with his old skill
of lifting up his one wide-bladed oar
the moment the cortege comes into sight.

Posthumous

After his death he appeared in dreams
to those who knew him most closely in life
and many times in every day
he crossed the minds of his wife and child.

But she grew old, the child grew up,
and he found his after-life falling apart:
the neural networks on which he depended
were being engrossed by later concerns.

But still there were words – those structures he'd built –
this bulwark against such wearing away;
and they held their own
and, after their kind, kept him alive –

until the invasion – its tide of new words.
His marks lost their meaning, and even the stuff
they were written upon disintegrated,
ground into featureless dust.

The Nimbus

I saw you walking outlined by a light
I took to be the old erotic fire –
the poet's motive manifest – desire
for the desirable. I was misled.
The nimbus shimmering around your head
was millions of cells your body shed
departing through the channels of your hair
to follow their existences elsewhere.
I was enlightened, helplessly, to see
the steady process of the setting free
of everything that makes you what you are,
the light the radiance of a fading star
whose substance will send out a final spark
long after being swallowed by the dark.

Roots

Eclogue: It was

to have mornings gladdened by milk churns,
a tuneless steel band;
to live within sound of water and bring in the cows
looking down on basking trout;
   I remember when the lorry shed its load
   the white bellies of dead fish.
to make the centrifuge whine as the cream and the milk
went their separate ways;
to break the portcullis of ice at the door of the barn
before the eyebrows congealed;
   I remember the rats inside,
   knocking them down with a broom.
to sit by the fire in a gale
protected by three feet of stone;
to lean on a wind as steady and solid as water
as if on a trusted friend;
   Don't you remember the flood –
   the body pulled out near the bridge?
to feel the tongue in the mouth
move with the curlew's cry;
to know where the irises grew, and the knees-bending
dipper nested each year . . .
   I remember
   the bull and the dry stone wall between them
   crushing the farmer to death.
to build a foursquare haystack
then slice it clean with the knife;
   I remember the dog's legs severed
   by that vicious mowing machine.
to leave and regret that wider
may never again be as deep.
   I remember the staunch chapel-goer
   and his pornographic collection.

   Live with your pastoral, brother.
   Let me keep a grip on the world.

A

Begins with A you say? It may be so.
She says she's certain we lay side by side?
Old men forget. It was so long ago.

With somebody I watched a white cloud grow,
but I can't place her . . . Did you say she cried?
Begins with A you say. It may be so.

I do recall a hayfield – row on row
half baled: we might have made ourselves a hide –
Old men forget. It was so long ago.

Or else there was a train – all puff and blow
pulling hard to get into its stride . . .
Begins with A you say? It may be so.

Or was there somebody's loud radio
announcing that some big-wig had just died?
Old men forget. It was so long ago.

She may now have five kids for all I know –
have been a nineteen-fifties blushing bride.
Begins with A you said. It may be so.
Old men forget. It was so long ago.

The Garden Revisited

The way the water flows
to this garden hollow shows

so our neighbour says, the land
is remembering a pond

which our predecessors tried
unsuccessfully to hide

because that's where their child had died.
Hearing this, our daughter cried

and now the meadowsweet grows there
its fragrance lingering in the air

whenever we three walk that way
to comfort . . . whom? we sometimes say

its dispersal is a sign
no urn could possibly confine

the essence of that little soul:
her part has now rejoined the whole.

The Meadow Remembers the Winter

The field on the other side of the valley
is greening –
the grass is starting to grow

but all the way down from the top run darkly
parallel lines
in row upon row

recalling the day when the meadow was crowded
as half the village
sledged in the snow.

The Fountain

Surging from the centre of the square,
the hissing column lofts, and lifts itself,
curves unendingly its bright, lithe back
over the high, invisible bar
and goes to pieces in its heady fall.

Spattering the blue slate of its base
it recollects itself, and pulses out
to drape its beady curtain round the rim
and lapse into a deep, unruffled pool.

And we, like everybody else, are drawn
to gaze at this expenditure of force
accepting its decline with sunlit grace
and rest awhile on the surrounding wall,
tempered by the touch of its chaste veil.

Lot 33

Just a northern street
cobbled and empty, moonlit
and lacquered with rain.

Roof

The corrugated asbestos of this long shed roof
keeps its harmful fibres well locked in
and every year thick pads of moss
cover up the sterile grey with green.

It has a hopeless long-term strategy
to be a layer on a forest floor.

But spring is nesting time. All local birds
know where to find the moss to line their nests:
they peck and scratch, and free more cushions
than all the nests in Lockley Wood require.
The rest roll off the roof to join the soil
or, left behind, start once again
the patient task of carpeting the roof.

Riding Home

She rides alone, attended by her fears.
The urban landscape that she travels through
is ugly, threatening, full of ears
and on the walls its vandalism leers
at decency like hers which still holds true.

An orange light appears and disappears
flashed on and off by a malicious crew
who coarsely twist her sweetness into sneers
which satisfy the more they misconstrue.
She rides alone, unconscious of their jeers

while they compete to keep her in full view –
more desperate as her destination nears
in case it holds some saving rendezvous.
What do they want? They want to force her fears
to pleasure their depravity with tears.

Man-made

Home

Did war erase your homeland off the map,
destroy your house and then rename your street?
No. Your town is listed in the index still.
Your language and the very way you speak it
are rooted in a certain place and family.
Mine was deemed to be inferior:
too many consonants, the Leader said.
I saw the pit he filled to make the point.

My accent now declares me out of place
and many of the English words I use
bring darkness with them, not your warmth and light:
for me a house is just a house.
Home is through a door inside my head.

The Island

At last – above the vague sea-roar
they heard waves breaking on a shore.
Immediately every man
in his delirium began
imagining what they would find –
surely a fertile island, kind
to sailors now so weak and thin
each face was like a death's head grin.

Ashore, they slept; but when they woke
(their sleep invaded by the croak
of carrion birds) delusion died:
detritus lay on every side –
plastic bags and bottles sunk
neck-deep in sand, long-lasting junk,
and worst of all, the fetid smell
from the land and from the swell
of carcasses, the easy prey
fatal to vultures in a day.
Waders and seabirds – all in time
were trammelled in a viscous slime;
and slowly they became aware
of a strange rattling in the air;
dry, rusty leaves, self-wounding knives,
fruitlessly laying down their lives.

Confronted by these sickening signs
they feared the poison had designs
on them, and none had any doubt:
better to push their frail boat out
and take their chance on the high seas
rather than die in scenes like these.

Prose Poem

You want your work to be topical? Don't mention today or a date. Keep it simple and short. For grammatical subject write "men, women and children". Draw their verbs, in the passive voice, from the rich lexicon of murder. Let the words await validation. They will not have to wait very long.

Calorific

How we welcome this dubious gift
   Prometheus stole from the gods.
No more killing cold in the winter:
   we tell stories, relax in the warmth.
Raw bleeding flesh our teeth used to tear
   peels tenderly now from the bone,
and when fire forged our metals life leapt
   to dig, and to prune, and to kill.
Ever since, our poets have flourished
   praising peace and the great deeds of war.
The flames kept the wild beasts at bay
   and made us more savage than them
for we are improvers on nature;
   we have taught the old dog some new tricks.
We call this machine gun to witness:
   little heat now goes a long way.
One spark can blow up a market:
   the shoppers are utterly changed.
We train fire to force up our rockets
   to land on the moon or a house.
One carried six astronauts piggy-back;
   they came down like a meteor shower.
The cynic finds proof for his mantra:
   "All blessings come with a curse."

Introduction

Welcome to our academy.
Remember that in everything you do
you serve a greater cause. At dawn each day
think how many lives you may well save
at the expense of one.
These quiet thoughts before the day begins
will send you to your work with more resolve.
Your aim, of course, is to preserve, not kill –
a principle we put to clever use
for often you can crown a good day's work
by bringing someone back when they seem gone.
Their disappointment is remarkable to see.

What follows is the Level 1 Module:
tools of the trade and the procedures
most commonly employed.
Promotion as you know is by exam –
two written papers and a practical.
Victims are provided.

Greenhouse Song

Spring Summer Autumn Winter –
Do you remember the round of the year
when day after day of monotonous sameness
was something we never thought we need fear –
Do you remember, dear?

Spring Summer Autumn Winter
are things of the past, and now we must all
brace ourselves for the future Sahara –
Does anyone living now recall
seeing snow fall?

Spring Summer Autumn Winter
with nature at rest, or in growth or decay –
in such sweet variation of season to season,
none of our children from now on will play.
Well-a-day, indeed! Well-a-day.

AD 3062

Ten years ago it started – nights in June
began to be unusually cool;
the water bowl we left out for the cat
by morning had a wafer-thin ice-lid.
So it went on, this retro-climate-change,
till legendary winters came again
with tunnels through drifts higher than the eaves.
Now even summer calls for central heating.
Believe me it's not fashion
that fills up every wardrobe with fur.
Those famous men who turned our ship around
are now disgraced in every history book:
they saved us from the tropics – now we freeze
and founder in these man-made, arctic seas.

Reading Ceramics

This pot kissed its neighbour in the kiln
and never forgot the experience.

★

Three Chinese brush-strokes –
a tree-bordered stream:
the economy of a drunken master.

★

Spout, handle, body, lid:
four letters
spelling teapot
so many ways.

★

White horses thunder around my bowl:
desperate, Phaeton is losing control.

★

To pick up this jug
is to catch a squirrel
by the tail.

★

(Made in Athens)	(Made in Sousa)
Noble Greeks	Noble Persians
kill cowering Persians.	kill cowering Greeks.

★

Time, like the fine glaze,
interposes
between us and the child
who painted roses
all day long.

★

Foolish, I know –
but when this jug swallows water
I look for the Adam's apple.

Solo and Chorus

Today is a landmark:
for the first time in our history
the prison population
exceeds those who are free.
(Let us hope the locks
are strong enough.)

Everyone with the slightest inclination
to commit the smallest crime
has been swept off the street.
Think of it before the refuse cart
empties the bins; think of it after –
all tidied away.
(Let us hope the walls
are thick enough.)

They've been thickened and heightened:
they shut out the sun till noon.
(May our good fortune ward off
earthquakes and subsidence.)

Old-fashioned broken glass has been replaced
by beautiful razor wire,
its gleaming coils six feet thick.
(Let us hope one fool's lacerations
are enough to deter the rest.)

The regime inside is severe
yet still they come back for more.
(Let us hope that repeated,
degradation changes their hearts.)

We have cut out creature comforts
and reintroduced uniforms.
Now they all look the same.
(Let us hope this teaches a lesson
that they've been too full of themselves.)

The whole prison service is run
by the thinnest of skeleton staffs.
As long as the inmates
remain locked in their cells
why should we the hard-working
pay warders for kicking their heels?
(Let us hope the prisoners are wise
in their use of this "thinking time".)

(What is the noise
washing over the walls?)
Rest assured.
Sleep well in your bed.
It is only the roar of impotent rage.

Bon Voyage

There was a farewell party, where they said,
"You'll only be a lowly crew member,
but seeing all the ports around the world,
getting to know the different ways of men,

will make you rich in life; you will be wise
and look forward so much to coming home --
to see your house again, your patient wife,
the old dog and the hens in the back yard."

Respectful of these elders he embarked,
excited by their words and older tales,
nostalgia a dull ache made bearable.

But he came home to find his house burnt down,
his wife a body in an unmarked grave,
the dog a feral creature scavenging.

The Purging Plain

We had to abandon the four-wheel-drive;
the tyres could get no grip on this terrain.
We'd gone beyond the land of the alive
and strayed on to the barren Purging Plain

where unknown weaknesses began to tell.
Surprisingly, at first it was the strong
who staggered drunkenly before they fell,
victims of some secret, hidden wrong.

Then one by one our party joined the dead,
leaving the rest of us to walk afraid
that no redeeming thing we'd done or said
would ever have sufficiently outweighed

our many ills. Caution was useless: overhead
the sword of justice trembled on a thread.

Personae

Hero

I hardly knew him when he came back – tanned,
stringy, more given than before
to silences.
He wouldn't say what happened to his friends
except that they had "dropped off one by one".
We know some threw his words back in his face
and then stampeded to a reckless death:
he had to stand aloof like an oak post
shuddering, and watch them swept away.

A storm at sea to him was just a test
from which he came off badged but proud.
And there'd been women too, but like a talisman
he'd held my mother's picture in his mind.
He spoke of monsters with a modest smile,
and out of suffering he made his songs,
so simple yet they wrung the listener's heart.

Who wouldn't want to emulate this man?
But when I spoke of leaving home myself
he urged me not to. "No, stay here," he said.
"The years will test your mettle just the same."

Crossing the Line

Every afternoon in junior school
when all our books were tidy in our desks
and all the rulers were accounted for,
Mr Barlow, whose name reminded me
of sugar sticks, would take his diary out
and read. He read about his days at sea
and, best of all, of how he crossed the line
for the first time – of how the crew dressed up
like monsters in a summer pantomime
and bundled him on deck to have a shave
and ducked him in cold water in a tub
while Neptune, in a Father Christmas beard,
supervised the ritual himself.
It clearly was quite heavy-handed fun
and yet he had enjoyed it all the same.
No other teacher brought the outside world
into the classroom as this Sinbad did
and when he spoke of jobs to do at home
boys volunteered to help him prune his trees.
I think that they imagined him aloft,
the nearest thing to Tarzan they had known,
and they were glad to pile his branches up
and feel him less a teacher than a friend.
He left quite quickly, we did not know why
though we suspected he'd been forced to go.
I bought an Oxo cube on my way home
and nibbled as I wondered what he'd done.

Satirist

There's nothing I like better than a fight –
aggressive couplets rolling off the tongue.
That's why my verse is always dynamite:
I sing no soppy art-for-art's-sake song.

I love impugning the sincerity
of all the politicians I deride
(you'd never guess that it enables me
to revel in my own egregious pride).

I make a bee-line for the highest ground
and then deploy my phoney indignation;
there's splendid satisfaction to be found
in moral denigration.

Of course, I never scruple to conceal
the many sins that blot my balance-sheet.
How else could I so righteously reveal
the hypocrite, the liar, and the cheat?

Poets have robbed and cheated and far worse
and then gone home to coin convincing lies
and set them down in everlasting verse.
So I'm a poet. What's the big surprise?

And when I land each verbal knockout blow
on all the biggest chins that you could mention
my greatest secret pleasure is to know
that I'm the real centre of attention.

Xanthippe

After his first wife died
he was all over me.
But not for long:
he now spends all his time
standing about
with hangers-on
and lounging with them
somewhere
half the night.
"Searching for truth"
he calls it.
From what I've heard
he ties them in knots –
asking questions,
questioning answers
till they agree with him.
Sometimes he starts on me.
I answer back:
"Hot air buys no cabbage –
That's the truth."
That's why they call me shrew.
Now he's up for trial.
You ask me what I think.
I tell you this:
he talks of his own ignorance
but when push comes to shove
he won't take back
a single word.
He'd rather die.
He'll not be home again.
Just wait and see.

Achelous

Desire drove him to change his shape –
First to a handsome serpent, showing off
The iridescence of his self-esteem,
Then to a bull in all his stiff-necked pride,
And finally to an ox-headed man
Whose beard, ending in pendulous green points,
Was conduit to an ever-running stream.
What woman might not see through this device
And then choose death disguised as Heracles?
What man would not do as the river-god?
What man knows any better what he brings?

Kanal

. . . we found ourselves in someone else's hell –
a circle even Dante had not seen.
This mole-dark tunnel streaming stench
was where we ate and drank and shat and slept
and spoke in lowered tones so long
I nearly lost my voice.
Here comrades somehow managed to admire
and fight over the women brave enough
to take with us the more than common risk.
Two children were born here, baptised in filth,
and after the delivery the women took their guns
and walked with gun and child on either hip.

They called us sewer rats, but never knew exactly
where we were – nor how we disappeared
after a strike.
They lobbed grenades which damaged walls.
Not us. We had our silent ways of killing.
After grenades they used their stinking guile:
the order to emerge was false – a lure
to have us all stand up to be gunned down.

What then am I – a ghost? No.
A miracle. Wounded, I acted dead,
and when they'd gone I crawled away
through spreading pools of all my comrades' blood.

Brave patriots took me in – tended me –
gave me the eighty years I have survived . . .

Foxy

He was handsome, no doubt about it.
The last time I saw him
was driving home late
from a department meeting.
I was stopped by the usual queue
and he walked across
as if he knew he was safe.

He'd been drawn to foxes as a boy –
slipped out of school to lie in wait,
too early he knew – but how could he miss
the thrilling anticipation.

When he chose photography we all expected
a safe career in food or fashion
but he traded in his camera
for the latest night vision
and took to his bed by day.

His mother noticed
the first sign of change: what she called
his "swivelling ears".

His camera was found
ruined by rain
on a new tripod.

As the traffic moved on
he whisked out of sight
the tip of his brush.

On the Front of The Radio Times

"Fame, infamy and me" –
what an indivisible three.
I think the serpent's main abode
is in our family tree.

Grampa taught me wickedness
when I was barely three:
he threw me up and caught me down
and sat me on his knee.

He made me chew tobacco;
I didn't like the stuff
but Grampa said, "Keep chewin' boy
– the juice'll make you tough."

So I chewed and chewed, and chewed and chewed
and then I learned to spit.
For target practice we used the cat.
I scored a direct hit.

I think the juice got in its eyes
'cause it jumped up and down.
But when I seemed to pity it
the old chap with a frown

said, "Drat! You pity nothin' boy:
ain't nothin'll pity you."
And I still recall his last remark
because it has come true.

"I hope for your old grandad's sake
you'll notch up enough crimes
to earn respect and see yourself
on the front of *The Radio Times.*"

Rats

A Still

It always greeted us when we came home
so when it wasn't there, we called and called.

We didn't know, but it was past replying:
a sandstone block had somehow been dislodged

and pinned the cat against the ditch's bank.
It couldn't draw the breath required for crying.

I found it in the morning, stiff in death,
a frame out of the zaniest cartoon.

Drought

We came across it when we'd lost our way,
a painful sight —
not of the dead, long since picked clean,
but of the one alive, the last of its kind,
reminding me heartlessly of nothing so much
as a toast rack on legs.

Its strings and sinews had long lost their power
leaving the bones to balance on themselves
like some child's game where players secretly delight
in waiting for a rattling collapse.
It did collapse, but softly, like the map we folded up.
Our water carriers were very low.
We had to find out where we were
or die.

Rat-hunt

Now we knew what happened while we slept:
a nightly impudent invasion
of rats. From gutters and the eaves they crept

out along the beams above the hens:
drawn by the food and water – plentiful supplies –
not in their ones and twos but in their tens.

When we slipped in and took them by surprise
and shone our torches on them through the dark
they froze. The cat's-eye glitter of their eyes

seemed to me to frame a nasty smirk –
wiped off their faces when they understood
our sticks and metal bars. We went to work

knocking them off – as many as we could –
on to the unyielding concrete floor
and stained it with small spots and pools of blood.

Hanging Out

Unlikely aviator! No goggles,
no helmet, no flying-suit;
more wonder still – no wings or tail
nor what one might expect to find instead,
some noisy means of moving through the air.

Yet thus apparently disqualified
you and your fellows' Cirque du Soleil
populate the Big Top of the sky
and glide on ropes sustained by weightlessness
just outside the range of human sight
yet not too far above the washing line
to land on the white platform of my shirt
and, challenged, abseil quickly to the ground.

Questions/
Divinities

Lucretius on Epicurus

O thou, the first to raise above the dark
a shining light to show life's benefits,
thou ornament of Greece – I follow you
and though I try to tread where you have trod
I am not emulous: I simply wish
to imitate you since I love you so.
Why should a swallow emulate a swan
or a young goat on shaky legs take on
the power and vigour of a thoroughbred?
You, Father, are the pioneer whose precepts
we imbibe, feeding on your pages
as bees sip nectar from the forest glades.
So likewise we take sustenance from words –
your golden words, worthy of immortality.
For straightaway, as soon as you declare
your reasoned explanation of all things –
the product of your godlike mind – my mind
loses all fear: the ramparts of the universe
give way, and in the void I see
the operation of all things. I see the gods,
their majesty, and their serene abode
where no wind blows, no clouds discharge their rain,
no frozen snow disturbs with white descent,
but where the ever-cloudless sky spreads over them
in smiling radiance, and for their peace of mind
nature continually supplies their needs.

The realms of Acheron I do not see
though notwithstanding earth I can look down
and see what lies beneath us in the void.

All this inspires me both with dread
and with divine delight – to know that by your power
the universe lies open to my gaze.

Prayer

Let us pray:
that the gods keep themselves to themselves;
that they never again take on flesh;

that they leave what is not well alone
and what is not clear they leave dark.

May they never bring things to perfection
least of all our fallible selves:

having made us recalcitrant
let them recognize what they have made.

Left alone, though we question and flounder,
sometimes we will put them to shame.

Truth is the Creation of the Word

Before language came on the scene
with words that are obliged to mean
only a wordless shout or cry
rose up into the silent sky
and everything – completely free
of "false" and "true" – need simply be.

Now humankind is caught
in the labyrinth of thought
and will be until mankind dies,
taking away its truth and lies
and all its words, each one replete
with the power of deceit.

Even then the world would strain
to be articulate again,
loving the truth, yet not denying
the versatility of lying.

A Blank Canvas

Although my brush is the creating Word
why spoil this perfect emptiness?
This light is good – Why ruin it with dark?
This nothing is obedient to my will –
no matter spinning out of my control.
There are no painful deaths, no pangs of birth,
no long sad slide of human history:
no slavery, no wars, no burning at the stake,
no codes of honour calling for revenge.
I can contain the whole sordid charade
by leaving this negation as it is.

And yet it is my nature to create –
The maker's joy outweighs darkness and death.

His loaded brush made the initial mark
and bad and good exploded into life.

Questions

Do you use language? Does language use you?
Shouldn't you try to be more aware?
How do you know what you're saying is true
and not, if language is using you,
just a distortion that filters through
so what you believe is what words say is there?
And if using language means it using you
how do you propose to be more aware?

Translations/
Derivations

The Blacksmiths (From the Middle English)

These soot-blackened blacksmiths with smoke-smeared
    faces
drive me to death with their bashings and bangings.
You never heard such a nocturnal cacophony
of loud-mouthed louts and continuous clatter.
The raucous rascals call for, "More coal! More coal!"
and puff up the forge with their brain-bursting bellows
huff puff from this side, haff paff from that.
The gangling sprawlers never stop shouting
and grunting, or groaning, or grinding their teeth
as they sweat over swinging their many-pound
    hammers.
A whole bull's-hide goes into making their aprons.
Their legs are gaitered to fend off the flinders.
Two taking turns, they put all their might
into heaving their hammers, and coming down heavy
on the anvil's block: lus bus, lus das, lus bus, lus das
keeping it up till you wish it to Hell.
The master lengthens a small piece, fashions a less,
twists them together and taps out a treble:
tick tack, tick tack, ticker tacker, tick tack.
Then it's bam again and bash again and bash again and
    bam.
That's how it goes. These horse-outfitters,
these water-trough-hissers – Christ send them sorrow!
Does no one deserve a damn good night's sleep?

Catullus 101

Brother,
I've come through many countries, over many seas
to be here at your grave, bring my last offerings,
and speak these words in vain to your mute ashes.

Poor brother, so rudely taken from me by your fate,
accept from me, as our ancestral rites ordain,
these sad gifts wetted with a brother's tears

and, brother, hail – this time for ever – and farewell.

Gallus

(after Propertius)

You – running wounded from the ramparts
    to escape the fate of the rest –
though I'm one of your closest comrades
    don't look back, red-eyed, when I moan.
Save yourself. Let your parents rejoice
    and no tears tell your sister my tale:
that all Caesar's swords couldn't kill me
    but some nobody did in the end.
Whatever bones she finds on the hillside
    let her not know them for mine.

Ronsard: from Les Derniers Vers

Long winter nights, my torturers, I lie awake
asking for patience and for sleep in vain.
Your very name makes my whole body shake
and sweat because you bring such cruel pain.

Sleep's wings don't even lightly brush these eyes;
the lids seem held apart – they will not close.
All I can do is utter my low cries,
suffering like Ixion eternal woes.

Old shadow of the earth or shade of hell,
forcing my eyes open with chains of steel
bringing bed-ridden me more injuries,
order Death to drive these ills away.

Our port and comfort, with joined hands I pray
Come Death – bury all my miseries.

Advice from Horace (a regurgitation)

Don't cast hopes into the future:
the odds are worse than in fishing.
Just school yourself to grin
and accept whatever occurs.

Whether this late spring snow
is the last you will ever see,
or the gods have a handful or more
to deal out to you one by one,

be advised. Time flies while we talk.
Grab it, and don't put your trust
in whatever is lurking ahead.

Tregiston (as from old Welsh)

My name is Tre-gis-ton, three forceful expulsions of
    breath.
Make sure you say it correctly. If you do you may live
    many years.
For I know where the grindstone is,
    and ash handles waiting for spears.
My stance is the bole of an oak; my walk is a rattle of
    quivers.
My arrows deliver a poison; my peacocks provide them
    with flights.
No axe goes rusty in my court, nor their wielders short
    of a job.

I am going to school in the future.
I will bring back an armourer's dream.
The sword will be seen in museums, a sign of how far we
    have come.

Though my sleep is like snow on the mountains
I have no need of metal or wood:
pure water – white milk – red blood
are enough to fuel my fire.
My crush is like a constrictor's
and my claws as fine as steel needles,
retractable on the outcrops,
leaping forth at the first smell of flesh.

My biceps are borrowed from bears;
one blow and men die like a blink.
I am furnished with fangs, once they close
say goodbye as quick as you can.
I play the moon like a cymbal, it resounds with my
    antlers' clash.
I am unicorn too ... Men say I'm a myth
till they watch their own blood drain away.

Do you understand what I'm saying?
The bright blade glitters in waiting.
Go down on your knees every day.